# Start Each Day With A Smile

A 5 Week Journey Of Self-Care, Self-Discovery and Personal Growth

Myra Wilkinson, LMFT

All rights reserved. No part of this publication may be reproduced, distributed, or transmitted in any form or by any means, including photocopying, recording, or other electronic or mechanical methods, without the prior written permission of the publisher, except in the case of brief quotations embodied in critical reviews and certain other noncommercial uses permitted by copyright law. For permission requests, visit www.mwilkinsonconsulting.org

Copyright © 2018 Author Myra Wilkinson, LMFT

All rights reserved.

ISBN: 0692178678
ISBN-13: 9780692178676

## DEDICATION

*To my family, friends, and clients; thank you for your inspiration, love and support.*

# CONTENTS

**INTRODUCTION**

**WEEK 1**     3

SELF- ESTEEM

**WEEK 2**     14

BOUNDARIES

**WEEK 3**     25

SELF- LOVE

**WEEK 4**     36

SELF-CARE

**WEEK 5**     47

PERSONAL GROWTH

**CONCLUSION**

*Thank you for allowing me to be apart of you self-care journey!*

# INTRODUCTION

## Getting Started

*Never Let Self- Doubt Hold You Captive – Ray Benndt*

START. Success will never happen without a starting point. There is no better time than the present to begin stepping in the direction of success. The elephant in the room that often gives us pause when trying to advance is seldom a lack of motivation. We desire success. We are motivated to succeed. Still, there is a stumbling block that trips us up, causing us to stop before we start. Self-doubt is the real culprit.

Being overly hard on ourselves can cause us to forfeit opportunities for happiness and success. As negative self-talk creeps in, we become defeated in our minds without having taken the first step toward change. Self-doubt and negative self-judgement work together to hinder personal growth. Happiness becomes a thing hoped for but never truly experienced.

Self-doubt can stem from past conflicts that have gone unresolved. Whether the negative comment came from a parent, family member, teacher, or peer, we carry these hurtful outside assessments and eventually claim them as our own. We begin to see ourselves through the lens of their negative judgments. Here is the freeing part: Their judgments do not have a right to define our truth.

Being told that we aren't good enough or smart enough to achieve success can cause those perceptions to become ingrained in us. Once we own these thoughts, they dictate our lives – defining who we are and the choices we make. Seeds of negativity that are planted at an early age have the ability to reproduce over and over again throughout our lives. These seeds are watered by unkind words, harsh criticism, and poor self-care. Glamorized images that society portrays as standards to live by add to the ever-mounting hurdle to be crossed. With thoughts and opinions coming from all directions, we become sidetracked, confused, and misguided. However, clarity is available. We can clear the clutter that dares to line our path to success. Introspection is how we start to take steps toward a successful, happiness-filled future.

How do you take back your life and regain control over the thoughts that are allowed to occupy your mind? What would happen if you choose not to let self-doubt holds you captive? What could you accomplish? What could you achieve? What is one thing you can do differently today that will release you from the captivity of self-doubt?

Perhaps you are currently at a loss for answers. That is perfectly okay. If the answers flowed easily, this experience wouldn't be a necessity. By the end of this journey, you will be able to smile and respond with confidence. Let's begin…

# WEEK ONE:
# SELF- ESTEEM

Self-esteem is one's attitude toward oneself. As I wrote and organized this chapter, I explored my thoughts and feelings regarding my self-esteem. I found great comfort in knowing that I have more power than I accredit myself. My hope for you this week is that you would find your place of comfort and for your self-esteem to begin growing in a positive direction.

– Myra Wilkinson

> *"As you reflect on your relationship you have with yourself, is this your ideal relationship?"* **- Myra Wilkinson**

Be honest. How well do you treat yourself? Before answering, consider that the following works against self-care:

Harsh comments about one's self
Poor eating habits
Lack of sleep/rest
Tolerating high levels of stress

How you value yourself sets the standard. In other words, the treatment of you by others is generally a result of how you treat yourself. By not making self-care a priority, the message is sent that you do not deem yourself as important. Ouch! The truth hurts, I know. However, truth is often the catalyst needed to shift our thoughts, words, and behavior.

Reflect on the relationship that you have with you. Is it ideal? Is this a healthy relationship or are there areas for improvement?

What message are you sending to others when it comes to how you treat you?

_____
_____
_____
_____
_____

START EACH DAY WITH A SMILE

***"Our personal qualities allow us to contribute something special to the world." – Myra Wilkinson***

Only you can be you. Society overloads us with images and ideas regarding how to look, what to eat, what to drink, and how to speak; thus, causing individuality to feel more like a burden than a blessing. Embracing your uniqueness requires courage and strength. Dare to be your own #1 fan! In doing so, you will tap into the tenacity needed to love and believe in yourself.

It is human nature to get sucked into the trap of comparison. As we measure ourselves against one another, we forget our values and our self-worth begins to diminish. The door swings open and self-criticism enters. Everyone – every, single individual on this planet – has something unique to offer the world. That includes YOU! There is something about you that stands out. You are an original.

Look in the mirror. What do you see? Ahhh. That is the reflection of a world changer. Live. Grow. Impact. See yourself for the irreplaceable individual that you are. Cultivate your gifts and share them with the world. Only you can be you. And the world needs you.

What are three qualities you love about yourself?

_____

_____

_____

_____

_____

START EACH DAY WITH A SMILE

## START EACH DAY WITH A SMILE

*"Doing what you love with the people you love is a privilege that should not be taken for granted." -Myra Wilkinson*

Make this declaration: Today is an amazingly good day! Now, say it like you mean it. TODAY IS AN AMAZINGLY GOOD DAY! Pause to consider the words that were just carried by your voice. Bask in that truth. Every day – as in every clump of 24 hours – has something magnificent to offer. Doing what you love with the people you love is a privilege that should not be taken for granted. Being able to find joy in each day is a beautiful experience.

Life is an adventure. It has twists and turns, ups and downs, leaps and falls. We make mistakes; we grow. We laugh, love and reflect. Rather than becoming frightened of the world's vastness, focus on the depth and width and height of you- the inner you. You are significant. On this amazingly good day (and every day) you are valuable. You have the privilege and honor of doing what you love with the people you love. Never take it for granted.

What is one dream that you haven't shared with others?

How will the fruition of this dream change your view on life?

_____

_____

_____

_____

_____

START EACH DAY WITH A SMILE

*"Fear is a funny thing. It robs us of a future, keeps us stuck in the past and makes us hide from the present." –* **Myra Wilkinson**

Fear is a funny thing. Anything – fear included – can be flipped on its side and viewed from a different angle. From one perspective, fear simultaneously robs us of hope for the future, cements us in the past, and causes us to presently shrink into the shadows rather than flourishing in our potential. That's life-stealing power! I challenge you to no longer view fear as a dirty word… as something to be, well, feared.

Let's flip fear on its side. Change your perspective. Rather than an excuse to stay stuck or a reason to not try the new thing, allow fear to be motivation. Make fear your reason for rising to conquer each day. Overcoming the very thing of which you are afraid qualifies you as a victor. Snatch the power of fear and use it to propel you forward.

Now, how do you view fear?

_____

_____

_____

_____

_____

_____

_____

_____

START EACH DAY WITH A SMILE

*"Self-love is the most beautiful gift you can give yourself. It allows you to be free and open. It allows you to love yourself so deeply that mere imperfections are no longer flaws but strengths."-Myra Wilkinson*

Feeling lost and uncertain are normal feelings with which we all wrestle. Burdensome thoughts arise to stop us in our tracks. Although our minds are the destination for those thoughts, their origins aren't always as easy to pinpoint. Maybe the negativity is arising from within, or perhaps darts of doubt from others are shaping our perspective. When too much merit is given to the opinions of others, we take their thoughts on as personal truth. What's the solution to maintaining a healthy view of life? Self-love.

There is no greater way to bless you than with self-love. Embracing you – flaws and all – causes strength to exude from within like never before. The freedom gained from loving self unconditionally opens your mind to possibilities that fear and doubt would have previously blocked. You are free to venture onto new paths because unconditional self-love breeds inspiration, motivation, and boldness.

For too long conditional self-love and the restrictive comments of those around you have infused your self-views with questions that barricade your abilities and self-worth. Self-love breaks those chains. Love you and be free!

What negative self-thoughts are currently preventing you from loving yourself deeply?

How would life be different if you were to love yourself unconditionally?

START EACH DAY WITH A SMILE

# WEEK TWO:

# BOUNDARIES

As I wrote this chapter, I was presented with the opportunity to explore my concept of boundaries. Upon completion, I learned that setting boundaries is something with which we all struggle. As we learn more about ourselves our boundaries change. This week I hope that you are able to discover what healthy boundaries are needed in your life to practice daily self-care.- Myra Wilkinson

***"Simply put, boundaries are the outlining perimeter of the spaces we fill with love and peace. These borders are established not just by word but by action also."-Myra Wilkinson***

As we come into a greater understanding of our needs and self-worth, we begin to explore the concept of healthy boundaries. Simply put, boundaries are the outlining perimeter of the spaces we fill with love and peace. These borders are established not just by word but by action also.

Frustration is experienced when the responsibility of our boundaries is placed on others, and they do not meet our expectations. We feel as though the ball has been dropped when they choose their needs over ours. Here is a helpful hint: You are responsible for setting your boundaries and ensuring that they are respected.

Your boundaries are a direct reflection of your values and self-worth. To set them is to draw a line in the sand and say, "My peace is a priority. My love is valuable. Positive energy is precious to me."

What boundary have you set verbally but not followed through with action?

_____
_____
_____
_____

## START EACH DAY WITH A SMILE

***"We give up too soon on opportunities that could change our lives because of fear of the unknown." -Myra Wilkinson***

Knowing when to hold on and when to let go are profound choices. Although decisions to grasp tightly or release freely may seem basic, they have enormous impact. Daily, we cling to things that are heavy and hurtful – be they thoughts, memories, or individuals. We accept being comfortable with dysfunctional familiarity because fear of the unknown has us bound.

And then there is letting go. Risking too much of ourselves may cause hurt, disappointment or embarrassment. Fear rears its head again, and we give up too soon. We bail on opportunities of a lifetime because we are unsure of how our lives will change. But change is good.

Coming to a place of balance requires time, energy, and a series of choices. Sometimes those choices are hard. Ultimately, you must find the power within yourself to hold on only to what's worth being held and let go of those things that dare to hold you back from experiencing a life of fullness and freedom.

What is one healthy thing you can hold onto?

_____
_____
_____
_____
_____
_____

START EACH DAY WITH A SMILE

> *"By holding on and not letting go we stay stuck in a circular pattern that tends to repeat itself until we learn to let go."- Myra Wilkinson*

The habit of holding on to hurt is hard to break. Holding on versus letting go or staying versus going is often a choice strongly tethered to an image of what is being lost rather than gained. Clinging to the familiar is normal. We often do so even at the risk of positioning ourselves for predictable hurt. The familiar, however unhealthy it may be, is still known and understood more than newness. Unfortunately, opportunities to learn and grow are forfeited when we stick to what's known.

Letting go creates space to experience better. Toxic relationships, negative feelings, and self-doubt clutter your atmosphere, leaving little room for the vast possibilities of greatness that await you. Holding on causes you to remain stuck in a circular pattern that will continue to repeat as often as allowed. This is your life. You have a choice. Admittedly, letting go of the familiar is scary and uncomfortable, but it is also well worth it. You deserve better than unproductive cycles.

What are you holding on to because of uncertainty?

What will you gain by letting go?

_____
_____
_____

## START EACH DAY WITH A SMILE

***"Letting go of the images that you must live up to is a complicated process."- Myra Wilkinson***

True freedom is experienced when success is no longer measured in numbers. What if the number of likes on social media no longer mattered or the scale didn't dictate your mood or the lack of commas on your bank statement wasn't such a big deal? Wouldn't you breathe just a little more easily?

Permit yourself to let go of the standards that hold you hostage. Dare to open your eyes to what is best for you then walk in the direction of "best". Deciding what to let go is empowering; letting go is the challenge. Exploring one's thoughts and feelings is the prerequisite for determining what is healthy and what is toxic.

Although a process, letting go is an accomplishment. Imagine the liberation experienced when wholeness-hindering factors are identified and severed. Think for a moment on how light your life would become if you would rid yourself of the unnecessary nouns – people, places, things, and ideas. Yes! You have the power to let go. You have the right to live your best life. What is one thing you can let go simply because it's heavy?

_____
_____
_____
_____
_____

START EACH DAY WITH A SMILE

*"Sometimes we lose our voice when we do not practice healthy boundary setting." -Myra Wilkinson*

"No" is a powerful word. It is the starting point of a balanced life and the means by which personal boundaries are constructed. No. No. NO! Become comfortable with this word for in it lies your power and your freedom.

It is often a struggle to say no to those for whom we care about. The need for boundaries is realized but saying no is a struggle. As a result of this unbalanced loyalty, we give more than we should and end up in an emotional deficit. Vulnerability, loneliness, self-doubt, and disconnection are a few of the repercussions of not setting boundaries. One minute we're giving, giving, giving and the next we are drained, irritable, and disengaged. Once this point is reached, it is difficult to retrace our steps to determine how we arrived at this point.

Deep exploration of our lives reveals that unhappiness is a result of personal choices. Without the power of "no," you will have no boundaries. Failing to set healthy boundaries allows the needs of others to outweigh ours. Building borders around your life, energy, and happiness send the message that you are important; your needs matter; your value is worth protecting. Thus begins the process of self-love and self-care.

Identify one boundary that can be put in place today to promote self-love and self-care.

_____

_____

_____

## START EACH DAY WITH A SMILE

# WEEK THREE:

# SELF- LOVE

Self-Love is the desire to cultivates one's happiness and wellbeing. I really enjoyed writing this chapter. I often smiled as I reflected on my love for myself. I explored negative cognition and choices that I have made. With this chapter, my self-love grew. I hope that as you explored self you, you find you and smile.

– Myra Wilkinson

*"Discover the things about yourself that you appreciate and love, then cultivate those things."-Myra Wilkinson*

Think about these things: What does it mean to live freely? What does it mean to explore the world without fear? How would life be impacted if your choices were made based on living rather than dying?

The answers to those questions vary from person to person. We all have perceptions that have been shaped by past experiences. For some, the world is their oyster, full of possibilities and potential. For others, the world is a cold, cruel place to be feared. How do we break free from debilitating messages that have been embedded in our souls? We start by choosing the messages on which we will focus.

Your beliefs are your decision. Create the life you want to live. Take chances; do new things; step outside the box. Discover the things about yourself that you appreciate and love, then cultivate those things. Freedom begins in the mind.

Identify one of your fears. What can you do to break free from that fear?

_____
_____
_____
_____
_____
_____

START EACH DAY WITH A SMILE

***"Every negative thought we allow to take up space in our minds decreases our opportunity to grow and does more damage to our self-esteem."*** *- Myra Wilkinson*

Think about what you're thinking about. Seriously, consider the dominant thoughts that turn over and over again in your mind. Every negative thought that we allow to take up space in our minds decreases our growth opportunities and does damage to our self-esteem.

Self-reflection often concludes that our thoughts didn't originate with us. Over time, the thoughts and opinions of others invade our thought life, thus giving them a level of control over us. If left unaddressed, being surrounded by negativity leads to unhealthy patterns and self-doubt. Our confidence decreases as we adopt other's opinions about who we are, what we have done, and who we are to become in the future.

Breathe easy; there is a remedy. You are responsible for your self-image. Yes! No one – absolutely no one – has the authority to negatively paint your self-perspective. You hold the key to how you view yourself. Your energy and your self-image are within your control.

What would happen if you committed to changing one long-held negative thought per day? What negative thoughts are preventing you from reaching your true potential?

START EACH DAY WITH A SMILE

> *"Once you begin to own your past, the present and future become that much brighter."*
>
> *-Myra Wilkinson*

The past is concrete. It is an indestructible facet of life from which no one is exempt. We all have a past, and we all can use the past as a healing-promoting mechanism. How so?

Holding on to past hurts causes us to get stuck. Our past finds its way into our present and future when our self-image is built around former poor decisions. We become mental prisoners to those choices, trapped in a negative cycle from which it is hard to break free. The power lies in perspective. Rather than holding on to hurt, examine it. Own your story. Embrace your past. Evaluate where you were, where you are, and where you are going.

The journey of life takes a positive turn when you learn to own your past. Mistakes were errors that gave way to learning experiences, correct? Think about it – growth came by way of conquered trials. Endings gave way to new beginnings. Once you begin to own your past, the present and future become that much brighter.

What parts of your past can you begin to own today?
How will owning a piece of your past change your present?

_____
_____
_____
_____
_____

## START EACH DAY WITH A SMILE

*"As we grow we learn to love ourselves more we explore the positive opportunities presented to us."- Myra Wilkinson*

Repeat after me: I am brave enough to love me. Say it again. I am brave enough to love me. Now, once more like you really mean it. I AM BRAVE ENOUGH TO LOVE ME! Wonderful job!

Loving yourself is to be an act independent of the thoughts and actions of others. It takes both courage and intentionality to love you beyond past mishaps. Yes, there have been less than favorable decisions made. Yes, you may still be grappling with the consequences of those decisions. Nevertheless, you are worthy of love.

Dig deep. Root out the "why" behind your actions. What would be the reason for making poor choices with no regard for the consequences that will follow? Perhaps feelings of loneliness, sadness, or insecurity play a role. Personal growth brings you to a place of self-love that causes positive opportunities to become appealing. Rather than falling prey to self-sabotaging cycles, self-love propels you toward better, healthier decisions. Self-love gives way to an increased sense of self-worth and frees you from the harsh judgments of others and yourself.

You are not bound by self-destructive behavior. You are courageous enough to break free. Allow self-love to break those chains.

As you deeply explore the core of who you are, identify one negative behavior that can be changed to promote self-love.

START EACH DAY WITH A SMILE

***"As we embark on the journey of self-growth and self-love, we learn to enjoy solitude as it is a time to connect with ourselves and learn how to appreciate our own uniqueness."*- Myra Wilkinson**

This will quite possibly push back against what is deemed to be right and proper. Brace yourself. Here goes. It is not selfish to focus on self. It is all too common of an occurrence that we place ourselves on the backburner. Our interactions with others become a distraction and a deterrent to getting our needs met. Yes, being connected to others can be life-giving. By all means, make healthy connections with others! But first, make time to connect with yourself.

To connect with you is to embark on a journey of self-discovery. What are your deepest needs and desires? Have you considered that you are both able and deserving of receiving grace and compassion that is turned inward? It's true! Forgive yourself. Be kind to yourself. Be considerate of your needs. Let's pause right there before moving on. Allow that to sink in. Forgive yourself. Be kind to you. Consider your needs.

In the solitude of intentional self-care moments is where you learn to appreciate your uniqueness. As you connect with yourself, you will begin to realize how valuable you truly are, which often prompts choices that promote growth. Connecting with you creates a positive flow of energy that helps to repel the negativity of others. Taking time to connect with you better equips you to connect with others.

How can you connect with yourself?
What can you do today to practice self-care?

## START EACH DAY WITH A SMILE

# WEEK FOUR:

# SELF- CARE

Compassion- What a power word! This was a very difficult chapter to write, however, I have grown through this process. My hope for you is that you grow as well!- Myra Wilkinson

*"Allowing other's decisions and choices to impact our lives is damaging. It takes away our ability to take care of our own needs."*- Myra Wilkinson

Balance must be established between self-sacrifice and self-love. True, to a great extent truly loving another person requires sacrifice; however, discretion must be built into the decision-making process. Could you by chance be carrying mountains that were meant to be climbed? Perhaps you are stuck shouldering the weight of someone else's dilemma.

Think about it. How often do you take on the weight of other people's problems? You mull over situations and formulate plans for how their crises can be averted. Before long, their poor choices have become your burden to bear. Your life is negatively impacted as a result. A compounding effect happens when you are left to handle personal drama in addition to that of those with whom you do life. There is only one you; you can only do so much. Refusing to be everything to everyone is okay. In fact, it's healthy.

What current mountain in your life can be climbed instead of carried?

How would this impact your life?

_____

_____

_____

START EACH DAY WITH A SMILE

***"As we yield to the pressure of people-pleasing, our authenticity becomes compromised."*** – Myra Wilkinson

How do you embrace who you are while catering to the images and expectations that others have placed on you? Is such a hybrid existence peacefully possible? Only you know those answers.

It is a common occurrence to sacrifice our self-care and self-love in an effort to make those around us happy. As we yield to the pressure of people-pleasing, our authenticity becomes compromised. Our true selves get lost in the tap-dancing routine of pacifying those for whom we have chosen to emotionally perform. Lean into this truth: You are unique. You are irreplaceable. Be unashamed about embracing the true you.

Life experiences often teach us to conform. We bend and blend to appease family and friends. Having the brave audacity to push back can potentially be met with let downs, misunderstandings, and heartache. However, not pushing back enslaves us to the opinions of others. The world is full of growth opportunities. These chances are hindered when the true you is prevented from emerging. Embracing the real, you create space for growth, improved confidence, and increase self-care.

Who are you?

_____

_____

## START EACH DAY WITH A SMILE

*"It is a gift to be able to bring happiness to others however as we pour into others we must first pour into ourselves"- Myra Wilkinson*

Neglecting to care for our personal needs creates barriers in life from which bitterness, exhaustion, and self-doubt can grow. We cannot give what we do not have. Compassion is no exception. To gift others with love and happiness, you must first gift yourself with compassion.

Without an understanding of your areas of growth, compassion for self cannot be exercised. Gautama Buddha said, "If your compassion does not include yourself, it is incomplete." Compassion is often only directed outward; however, healthy is the one who has grown to the point of directing it inwardly as well. Compassion for self is a key component of self-care that cultivates love, kindness, and peace. These attributes begin inward and radiate outward.

What can you do today to practice self-compassion?

_____
_____
_____
_____
_____
_____
_____
_____

START EACH DAY WITH A SMILE

## "We find ourselves unhappy and feeling disconnected- we become overwhelmed."- Myra Wilkinson

STOP! Yes, previously the advice was to START, but now stopping is imperative. It is normal and even widely encouraged to plan for tomorrow, but what about today? Let us not forget that today is packed with possibilities and experiences that may not come back around. And then there is yesterday! Much of our mental sight is spent glancing backward. Mistakes made, people wrong, and opportunities missed bombard the forefront of our minds. Again, what about today?

Pause in the now. Find time to be happy and enjoy the small things that are typically taken for granted. Take pleasure in discovering moments of bliss in the mundane. Practicing happiness doesn't have to be a chore. True, it is a weekly struggle to create balance and make time for self-care. The last thing we want is to add to our ever-growing to-do list, even if that addition is "make time for happiness". Wait. Why not? Pausing to search deep within usually reveals that we are not taking care of our personal needs. Perhaps the issue is inadequate sleep or not taking time to acknowledge what we have and how far we have come.

We are worthy of self-care. We deserve the opportunity to stop and smell the roses. Most likely no one will force us to practice self-care. Instead, we must choose to bless ourselves by taking time to live in the moment.

What would happen if I stopped to acknowledge my surroundings – the people, places, and things that form my world?

How can I make me a daily priority?

_____
_____
_____
_____
_____
_____
_____
_____
_____
_____
_____
_____
_____
_____
_____
_____
_____

Insert your own quote.

_____
_____
_____
_____

Today, let's take time to reflect on self-care. In this space cultivate what insight has been gained and the growth that you have experienced.

_____
_____
_____
_____
_____
_____
_____
_____
_____
_____
_____
_____
_____

## START EACH DAY WITH A SMILE

# WEEK FIVE: PERSONALGROWTH

Personal growth is a lifelong journey- as it should be. If we do not grow, we stay stagnate and miss out on opportunities that could lead to our greatest blessings. This chapter was organized last in this book because it is my hope that by now you are at a place in your journey that you can appreciate and embrace who you are and where you are going.

– Myra Wilkinson

*"Whether an experience is positive or negative, the opportunity for growth is present." Myra Wilkinson*

Growth is to life as sunlight is to a plant. Personal growth – the on-going evolution of you – is the spice of life and the hope for tomorrow. It is increasing the capacity of your character and the boldness of your brilliance. Growth is the option to begin again… as often as needed. Where you are isn't where you will always be. Look inward; branch outward; make new strides. Carpe diem!

Each new day is packed with the potential of discovering something new about yourself, others, and the world around you. Understand that negative experiences do not have to produce negative outcomes. Find the silver lining. We are so prone to zero in on the negatives that we overlook the positives. Thus, growth is hindered; be it personal, interpersonal, or career-wise.

I challenge you to not fixate on the missing pieces. All things may not be as you wish they were but find contentment in the things that are as they should be. Step back, breath, and look again. The rest will come into alignment as a new outlook is adopted. View disappointments as learning opportunities. Whether an experience is positive or negative, the opportunity for growth is present.

Reflect over the last year. What growth have you experienced? How has your life been impacted because of it?

START EACH DAY WITH A SMILE

## START EACH DAY WITH A SMILE

***"The beauty of a curveball is the joy you feel when you hit it!"*-Myra Wilkinson**

Curveballs will come. That's a fact of life. Calm down. Don't stress. There are ways to decrease the likeliness of being overcome by the unexpected. Learning to be comfortable in your own skin, developing healthy communication habits, and exploring growth opportunities are a few ways to do just that. Committing to personal growth causes victories to be built into everyday life. Progress is a serious accomplishment! As negative cycles are broken, you become happy with whom you are becoming, perspective shifts. Life's trials no longer seem insurmountable. The approval of others becomes less important. How so? It's simple – you are your own cheering section.

Rejoice for you! Your journey is *your* journey. It does not have to be dictated by the opinions of others or predicated on their approval. One's inability to acknowledge your evolution reflects their lack of growth rather than yours. Their unwillingness to see beyond the old you has no right to hinder your process. Keep going; keep growing! As curve balls come – and they will – knock them out of the park!

What self-growth has been recently stopped due to the negativity of others?

What can be done this week to promote self-growth?

START EACH DAY WITH A SMILE

*"Exploring all areas of our lives and taking in the world around us helps to promote personal growth." -Myra Wilkinson*

As sure as the clock keeps ticking, change will continue to take place with or without your permission. The reality is that while change is undeniable, personal growth is a choice. Each new day affords us the opportunity for new experiences. Take a different route to work; strike up a conversation with a stranger; try a new food. Exploring all areas of our lives and taking in the world around us helps to promote personal growth.

Growth is a common aspiration, but many fail to take the necessary steps to break out of their comfort zones. It is to be assumed that challenges prevent happiness and success. Thus, we conclude that life's hurdles impede growth. On the contrary, growth is a result of welcoming challenges, breaking through barriers, and choosing to do what you have never done before.

What does personal growth look like for you?

_____

_____

_____

_____

_____

_____

_____

## START EACH DAY WITH A SMILE

***"Through service, I was able to reconnect and find pieces of myself that had either been long forgotten or never discovered." – Myra Wilkinson***

As a matter of fact, participating in activities that benefit others stimulates self-growth. There is an element of fulfillment built into giving yourself to a cause to which you feel strongly. I recall having experienced such an opportunity. Through service, I was able to reconnect and find pieces of myself that had either been long forgotten or never discovered. Imagine that! I found me when turning my focus toward others. To be in the moment and acknowledge your presence in this great, big world is an indescribable feeling that we don't pause to experience often enough.

Slow down. Take in your surroundings. Create space for opportunities that would be generally missed in the day-to-day rush of life. Some of my happiest moments are when I can give myself *and* find myself at the same time. Go ahead. Try it! I'm sure you'll find it rewarding as well.

What might be discovered if you were to intentionally reconnect with yourself?

How can rediscovering pieces of you lead to growth?

_____

_____

_____

_____

START EACH DAY WITH A SMILE

***"Growth is a personal internal experience that constantly evolves into new levels of liberation."-***
***Myra Wilkinson***

Freedom is as unique of a concept as those who conceptualize it. For some freedom is a flexible work schedule or ample amounts of leisure time. To others, it is being able to make choices without negative consequences. But what does freedom mean in terms of growth?

Growth is a personal internal experience that constantly evolves into new levels of liberation. Our perspective of growth varies based on our position in life. For all, growth is a measurement of freedom. It is the freedom to be true to you while making choices that bring personal happiness as long as others aren't hurt by those decisions. Growth reminds us that we are not our past. Lessons learned are the product of past choices that were less than favorable. Thus, growth is experienced, and we become free from guilt and shame. Freedom is attainable.

What growth have you experienced in the last 6months? What lessons have you learned and how do you apply them daily?

_____
_____
_____
_____
_____

## START EACH DAY WITH A SMILE

# Conclusion

As we end this 5 week journey of self-care, self- discovery and personal growth, I hope that you will cultivate the growth that you have gain from this experience and continue to practice self-care and reflect daily on your actions and choices. I will continue to practice self-care and you can follow my journey at www.mwilkinsonconsulting.org.

www.ingramcontent.com/pod-product-compliance
Lightning Source LLC
Chambersburg PA
CBHW031256110426
42743CB00039B/612